T AXIS ·· LOOKING NORTH

SECTION ON E & W AXIS
SECTION THRU WORK SPACE

JOHN G. SHEDD AQUARIUM
·CHICAGO · ILLINOIS·

APPROVED   AUG 2ᴺᴰ 92?   COMM 5:47

13

SCALE AS NOTED

GRAHAM, ANDERSON, PROBST & WHITE ARCHITECTS
CHICAGO   ILLINOIS

SHEDD
AQUARIUM

SHEDD AQUARIUM

THE FIRST 75 YEARS

KAREN FURNWEGER

TEHABI BOOKS

CELEBRATE
75 SHEDD
AQUARIUM

PART ONE

Mr. Shedd's Gift

9

PART TWO

Chicago's Inland Sea

23

PART THREE

Neptune's Temple

41

PART FOUR

The World's Aquarium

53

1

PART ONE

MR. SHEDD'S

GIFT

Far left: The aquarium's steel skeleton shows the beginnings of the octagonal dome and vaulted galleries.

Left: The elaborate bronze front doors are surrounded

with marble and topped with an intricate, realistic sculpted reef scene.

Opposite: A busy day in the 1930s

Shedd Aquarium's great bronze doors swung open to the public

for the first time on December 19, 1929. Chicagoans had dug out from a blizzard just two days before, and they would be burdened for years to come by the stock market crash that had occurred two months earlier. A sneak preview of the new public aquarium—the world's largest—was a much-needed tonic. Only one exhibit, the tropical pool in the rotunda, was filled with animals. Yet people came in throngs throughout the holiday season to see the marble halls, skylight dome, and bronze fixtures. This gorgeous building was theirs, and they embraced it. In 1931, the year the final exhibit room was opened, Shedd Aquarium welcomed a record 4.69 million visitors.

As of 2005, more than eighty-nine million people have enjoyed a day of aquatic adventures at Shedd. Still the world's largest indoor aquarium, it is home to more than twenty-one thousand animals representing fifteen hundred species of fishes, invertebrates, amphibians, reptiles, birds, and marine and freshwater mammals. Shedd is a leader in the international zoo and aquarium community and is known for its exhibits, animal care, and educational programs. It is even home to "Granddad," a fish still on exhibit that was acquired to wow the crowds at the World's Fair held in Chicago in 1933.

For three-quarters of a century, Shedd Aquarium has been a Chicago icon. Its great history began with an extraordinary gift to the city.

An Aquarium for Chicago

On January 24, 1924, John Graves Shedd, retired president of Marshall Field & Company, donated two million dollars to build the world's largest aquarium for the people of Chicago. Shedd was among a group of civic-minded business leaders who strongly supported the young city's cultural growth. A self-made millionaire, he believed that "too many men have made fortunes in Chicago and while making them have left the city to grow as it would."

In order to bequeath a lasting gift to Chicago, he consulted with his peers. Together, they determined that every great city in the United States and Europe had a fine aquarium. Chicago must have the best. Shedd imagined a stately marble building and a collection of aquatic animals from around the world that would complement the two world-class institutions already in Grant Park—the Field Museum and the Art Institute of Chicago.

On February 11, 1924, the not-for-profit Shedd Aquarium Society was founded to construct, maintain, and operate the aquarium. On the society's fifteen-member board was James Simpson, who had succeeded Shedd as president of Marshall Field's. Shedd gave Simpson the task of overseeing the construction of the aquarium. Simpson was a key figure in the city's progressive urban planning movement and a skillful negotiator who paved the way for most of Chicago's public building projects in the 1920s and 1930s.

Even before Shedd's intentions were made public, Simpson got an enthusiastic, no-strings-

attached go-ahead from Chicago mayor William Hale "Big Bill" Thompson, a victory considering Thompson's administration was known more for its corruption than for its public works. Simpson then quickly arranged to have the South Park Commission, which later became part of a unified Chicago Park District, donate the circle of landfill it owned at the foot of 12th Street (now Roosevelt Road). He also hired the architectural firm of Graham, Anderson, Probst & White—the best in the Midwest at the time—to design the building. Meanwhile, Shedd's new director, George F. Morse Jr., lobbied the Illinois General Assembly to approve legislation enabling the South Park Commission to levy a small tax—similar to funding given to Chicago's other museums—to maintain the new aquarium.

Shedd Aquarium has nearly doubled in size, growing from 225,000 square feet when the original building was completed in 1929 to 422,000 square feet with the addition of the Oceanarium and Wild Reef.

In September 1925 the Shedd Aquarium Society entered into contracts with John G. Shedd and the South Park Commission to build and stock a "high-grade aquarium," and Shedd wrote a check for two million dollars. A year later, when rising costs threatened to scale back the size and quality of the building, he increased his gift to three million dollars, allowing construction to continue unchanged.

Lincoln Park Aquarium

In 1924 Chicago already had a new aquarium, which had been added to the Lincoln Park Zoo the year before. One of only seven public aquariums in the country at the time, and at seventy-five hundred square feet the largest freshwater aquarium in the world, Lincoln Park drew about two million visitors a year. It featured an extensive collec-tion of North American fishes as well as tropical freshwater species. The basement of the handsome brick building also held a fish hatch-ery that produced thirty million fry—including salmon—and several varieties of trout, whitefish, and pike to be released into Lake Michigan and other northern Illinois waters each year.

The Lincoln Park Aquarium closed in 1936. Overshadowed by Shedd, it suffered from a lack of funds as the Great Depression dragged on. Moreover, it had been ordered by the Board of Health to clean all the water it pumped from the lake by treating it with chlorine, which spelled disaster for the fishes.

PART DETAIL ELEVATION OF WEST WALL OF OCTAGON HALL Scale 3/8"=1'0"

SECTION THRU OPENING Scale 3/8"=1'0"

Left: The hatchery in the aquarium's basement was the main source of game fish for northern Illinois lakes and streams.

Below: On the main floor of Lincoln Park Aquarium, guests admire a trout exhibit, part of the country's finest trout collection in the 1920s and 1930s.

Opposite: The graceful brick building at Lincoln Park Zoo was the world's largest freshwater aquarium when it opened in 1923.

Shedd gratefully accepted Lincoln Park's entire collection of approximately four hundred fishes. Shedd donated a matamata turtle when Chicago's original public aquarium reopened in 1937 as the Reptile House. Since 1998, the building has served as the zoo's café.

The Merchant of Chicago

His name is chiseled in stone over the entrance to the aquarium. But who was John Graves Shedd? According to his boss, Marshall Field, Shedd was "the greatest merchant in the United States." As vice president of Marshall Field & Company, Shedd ran Chicago's famous department store. After Field died in 1906, Shedd succeeded him as president of the company, a post he held until he retired in 1923, when he became chairman of the board of directors.

Under Shedd's leadership, Marshall Field's grew from the largest store in Chicago to the largest wholesale and retail dry-goods business in the world. In 1907 Shedd replaced the State Street store—built in the 1870s—with a luxurious modern building that boasted thirty-five acres of selling space. The structure, which is still Marshall Field's flagship store, was designed by Ernest A. Graham, who would later design the aquarium as well as serve on its board.

Clearly, Shedd knew how to direct a successful business. Yet this great businessman came from humble beginnings. John G. Shedd was born in a low frame farmhouse in Alstead, New Hampshire, on July 20, 1850. The youngest of eight children, he turned his back on farm work when he was sixteen and set his sights on a business career. He worked at several dry-goods stores in Vermont and New Hampshire, earning positions of increasing responsibility and saving most of his modest income. At night, he read textbooks to further his education. By 1872, Shedd was ready for greater challenges and rewards than small-town New England could offer. In August of that year he headed west to Chicago to work for "the biggest store in town."

It was less than a year after the Great Fire of 1871 had leveled most of the city, and Chicago was rebuilding quickly. For an ambitious, imaginative young man, Chicago was a city of opportunity. Shedd walked into the Field, Leiter & Company store on State Street and asked Marshall Field for a job. As Shedd would later recount, Field asked the young man what he could do. "Sir, I can sell anything," he replied with confidence. Field hired him as a ten-dollar-a-week salesman and stock boy with a note to his supervisor to raise his weekly salary in six months "if suits" or "let him go at any time if does not suit."

In 1985 John G. Shedd was elected posthumously to the National Freshwater Fishing Hall of Fame in the category of Organization and Education. The Wisconsin organization cited Shedd's generous funding of a "world-class aquarium committed to education about the aquatic environment."

Shedd, whose rural New England background and earnest work ethic matched Field's, "suited" very well: Field raised his pay three times in the first year. Within the store's large wholesale operation, Shedd advanced to head of the important laces and linens department and then to general manager of the entire wholesale business. In 1893 he was made a partner in the company, and in 1901 he became vice president under Field himself.

Shedd had a strong sense of civic responsibility. He began the store's tradition of public service to the community. For his employees, he established a branch of the Chicago Public Library at the store, along with a gymnasium and a junior academy that allowed young workers to earn the equivalent of a high school diploma. Because he had had no source of good books as a boy, he donated a library to his hometown of Alstead. And he gave generously to his adopted city, donating tens

of thousands of dollars to the University of Chicago, the Art Institute, and the YMCA. Shedd was a member of the Commercial Club of Chicago, which commissioned Daniel Burnham's visionary 1909 Plan for Chicago—the now-famous Burnham Plan—and was appointed to the Chicago Plan Commission to put it into effect. Charles H. Wacker, chairman of the commission, said, "Mr. Shedd's interest in the Chicago Plan never flagged. He took great satisfaction out of the plan improvements, as they were realized one by one, for no one understood better than he their significance in the life and growth of the city he loved."

The centerpiece of the Chicago Plan was the lakefront, and here Shedd made his greatest contribution: the aquarium. Yet he never saw more than the architects' first

John G. Shedd's widow, Mary R. Shedd, gave generously to the aquarium, especially during the lean years of the Great Depression. Shedd's daughters, Helen Shedd Reed (later Helen Shedd Keith) and Laura Shedd Schweppe, contributed four hundred thousand dollars early in 1930 to help purchase the animal collection. Mrs. Keith also provided for the Aquatic Education Center, which opened in 1975.

drawings. Shedd died of complications from appendicitis on October 22, 1926. Just ten days earlier, as he left his office at Marshall Field's, he had expressed his desire to see the aquarium completed.

His death was front-page news, and on the day of his funeral, store employees were given the day off to honor the slight, white-haired man who had told them, "I would like you to remember that this store is only what the people of Chicago, the West, and the nation have made it. It was founded to render a public service."

John G. Shedd was buried in Rosehill Cemetery on Chicago's North Side. Thirteen months later, ground was broken for his aquarium.

2
PART TWO

CHICAGO'S
INLAND SEA

23

Far left: In early 1926 Shedd's associate director, Walter H. Chute (center), and Mario J. Schiavoni (left), project designer for Graham, Anderson, Probst & White, set off on a tour of West Coast aquariums. Pictured with them is Shedd's first director, George F. Morse.

Left: The original tropical pool in the rotunda was based on similar features in European aquariums.

Opposite: A page from Chute's small leather trip notebook contains sketches of the then-new Steinhart Aquarium in San Francisco.

Creating the world's largest—and finest—aquarium more than one

thousand miles from any seacoast required three years of research and careful planning. After forming the Shedd Aquarium Society in 1924, John G. Shedd and the society's directors hired George F. Morse Jr., former director of the Boston Zoological Park, the South Boston Aquarium, and the brand-new Brookfield Zoo, to be the director of the new aquarium. The next year, Morse recruited Walter H. Chute, his successor at the Boston Aquarium. Shedd and James Simpson were impressed with Chute and appointed him associate director.

More than anyone else, Chute influenced how the aquarium looks and operates today. Traveling with an engineer from Graham, Anderson, Probst & White, he toured the leading aquariums in Europe to study their design, construction, and management during October and November of 1925. The men also visited aquariums in New York, Boston, Philadelphia, Detroit, and San Francisco. Chute made detailed notes and sketches in a small loose-leaf notebook.

Back in Chicago, he worked side by side with the architects to incorporate the best of the classic designs with state-of-the-art water filtration systems, spacious work areas for the animal-care staff, and wide viewing spaces for aquarium guests. Shedd and the society board approved the first sketches for the aquarium in the fall of 1926, just weeks before Shedd's death. Plans were completed in July of 1927 and construction began on November 2, 1927. In 1928 Morse resigned, and Chute was made director, a post he held for thirty-six years.

San Francisco Aquarium.

Situated in beautiful Golden Gate Park. Built by private bequest. Maintainance by city - controlled by Cal. Academy of Sciences. Center building of a group of three, two of which are completed. Court yard in center of group with three out door pools for seals and sea-lions.

Entrance opens into a very attractive tropical swamp. Three entrances lead from swamp room to main exhibition hall. No provision made to control crowds. Difference of opinion among the staff as to the efficiency of this arrangement.

Floor of entrance and main hall set with soft tile with an occasional figure of crab, sea horse etc. Shows serious signs of wearing although

The building was completed in two years. But the projected October 1, 1929, opening date came and went due to delays in getting tank materials, life-support equipment—and salt water, which had to be shipped in railroad cars from Key West, Florida. When the first five-car shipment arrived on December 10, Shedd Aquarium Society president Melvin A. Traylor announced that the rotunda would be open to the public on December 19. "The public must understand, however," Traylor cautioned, "that the exhibition tanks proper are not yet ready and that for the present, the display of marine life will be very limited."

In fact, the only display was a forty-foot-diameter freshwater pool in the rotunda, featuring native fishes, reptiles, amphibians, and tropical plants. Even after the vast reservoirs were filled with seawater and the water-circulation systems were running, the new concrete tanks had to stabilize chemically before any marine fishes could be brought in.

Collecting finally began in the spring of 1930, the first of what would become two major collecting trips a year. On May 30, 1930, the first of the six galleries officially opened in a ceremony attended by Shedd's widow, Mary R. Shedd, and other family members. The final two galleries opened five months later—after 160 railroad cars of salt water had been delivered—in October of 1930.

The balanced aquarium room, featuring small freshwater exhibits similar to home aquariums (later renamed Tributaries), opened on June 1, 1931, and signaled the full realization of John G. Shedd's intentions. Shedd Aquarium not only housed the greatest variety of sea life under one roof—at the time exhibiting 5,000 animals, representing 400 to 450 species—but it was also the first inland aquarium to maintain a permanent exhibit of marine and freshwater fishes, from both the Atlantic and Pacific Oceans. It was also the first to devote an entire room to the display of balanced aquariums.

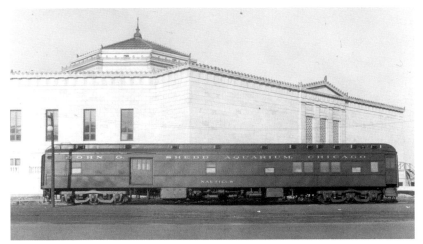

Gathering the Collection

Shedd Aquarium collecting trips are a tradition that dates from the earliest days of the institution. At first, collecting was a necessity: Many exotic species were not available through wholesalers or by trading with other aquariums. Today, collecting continues to be an important method for Shedd to obtain its unique display of aquatic life from around the world.

Traveling with *Nautilus*

Most of the first marine fishes on exhibit arrived on the *Nautilus*, a Pullman train car custom-built for long-range collecting trips. Before the days of air-freight, Shedd could not have maintained its saltwater collection without this railroad car. From its maiden trip to Key West in April 1930 until it was retired in 1957, the *Nautilus* traveled approximately twenty thousand miles a year to Maine, Florida, California, and even to the Midwest. Built by Pullman Car Works in Chicago for about thirty thousand dollars, the *Nautilus* was fitted with tanks, pumps, air compressors, electric refrigeration coils, and steam heat for an additional ten thousand dollars. It could accommodate cold and tropical saltwater fishes and cold, temperate, and warm water species. During the aquarium's first four years, the *Nautilus* transported more than twenty-one thousand fishes, mostly tropical marine species. Walter H. Chute called it "a miniature traveling aquarium."

Two-thirds of the eighty-three-foot car was allocated to life-support equipment and tanks—sixteen two-hundred-gallon waterproof cypress boxes that rolled on and off the car and twenty thirty-gallon metal containers. The remainder of the car was outfitted to serve as simple living quarters for the six-person

Far left: An 1873 engraving depicted an unlikely display of marine life.

Left: The interior of Detroit's Belle Isle Aquarium, built in 1904, resembles Shedd's original galleries.

The Dawning of the Age of Aquariums

The Victorians of the mid-nineteenth century were fascinated with the natural world that global exploration was opening up to them. Zoos were wildly popular, and once people understood how to care for aquatic animals, large-scale exhibits of never-before-seen marine life became the rage.

The term "aquarium" first appeared in the writings of Philip Gosse, a nineteenth-century English naturalist. Gosse helped establish the first public aquarium at the London Zoological Society in 1853. At first, the aquarium-building boom was limited to coastal cities with ready access to seawater. Gosse solved that problem by adding a combination of sea salts to clean freshwater, a procedure still used by inland aquariums today. England's Brighton Aquarium, the largest in the world when it opened in 1872, displayed dolphins, sharks, sea turtles, and scores of fishes. By the early 1900s, there were aquariums from Paris to Tokyo.

In 1856 P. T. Barnum opened the first aquarium in the United States in New York City. In 1873 the nation's first public aquarium, National Aquarium in Washington, D.C., opened in Woods Hole, Massachusetts. It was moved to the Washington Mall in 1888 and has been housed in the U.S. Department of Commerce building since 1932. Soon aquariums sprang up around the country: New York Aquarium in 1896; Waikiki Aquarium in the territory of Hawaii and Belle Isle Aquarium in Detroit in 1904; Point Defiance Zoo and Aquarium in Tacoma, Washington, in 1905; Memphis Zoological Garden and Aquarium in 1906; South Boston Aquarium in 1912; Steinhart Aquarium in San Francisco and Chicago's Lincoln Park Aquarium in 1923; Columbus Zoo's aquarium in 1927; Shedd Aquarium in 1930; and Dallas Aquarium in 1936. It took the global economic crisis of the 1930s, followed by World War II, to bring the great wave of aquarium building to an end.

collecting crew, with bunks, a bath, and a kitchen. Fully loaded, the *Nautilus* carried forty-five hundred gallons of water. But the seawater that sloshed during the April-to-November collecting seasons and exposure to the elements during winters spent in the Illinois Central Railroad yard eventually took a toll. In 1957 the rusted car was taken out of service.

With no long-distance collecting trips that year or the next, some of the saltwater exhibits were empty as the board searched for an affordable replacement. They found it in a retired stainless-steel lunch car, which they purchased and had refitted by the Thrall Car Manufacturing Company for a total of $175,000.

Two Shedd grandsons, John Shedd Schweppe and John Shedd Reed, served on the aquarium's board of trustees, the latter as president of the board from 1984 to 1994, overseeing the Oceanarium project.

Hitched to a high-speed passenger train, the *Nautilus II* made its first run to Florida in May 1959 for a collecting trip to Bimini in the Bahamas. That car reached the end of its line in 1972, the victim of deterioration and discontinued routes. In 1975 the *Nautilus II* was donated to the Monticello Railway Museum, near Champaign, Illinois, where it is on exhibit and open to the public.

Coral Reef Collections

By the time the second railroad car was retired, several factors were already changing the way the aquarium collected fish. Airfreight was becoming a

Opposite: Walter H. Chute devised a recipe for artificial seawater that could be made in limited batches.

Right: A workman pumps fresh seawater from railroad tank cars into the aquarium's reservoirs. It took 160 carloads—carried by twenty tank cars circulating between Chicago and Key West—to deliver one million gallons of salt water for Shedd's exhibits and reservoirs.

Filling the Inland Sea

In early 1930 one million gallons of ocean water were moved sixteen hundred miles by rail from the Florida Keys to Grant Park and pumped into Shedd's massive reservoirs. Although synthetic salt water was available, aquarium officials had chosen natural seawater, which guaranteed the proper salinity. To complete the task, the aquarium borrowed twenty insulated railroad tank cars from the Union Tank Car Company. Commonly used to transport gasoline, the cars were cleaned and lined with wax to prevent contamination. The insulated cars maintained the 75°F water temperature to keep the natural microscopic marine life in the water alive. The shipment cost about fifty thousand dollars, or four cents per gallon.

Over the years, both natural seawater and a synthetic mix—a combination of lake water and eleven sea salts devised by Walter H. Chute—replaced day-to-day water losses. In November 1970 a barge carrying eight hundred thousand gallons of seawater from

Shedd Aquarium Formula · Artificial Sea Water.

Absolute Salt percentage Required	Use:	Grams.	Absolute Salts obtained Total Grams.	Ultimate Analysis % of Residue
$NaCl$ - 77.70	"K.D. Anchor" Brand Granular Salt. (99.67% NaCl.) *Morton Salt Co.*	10,905.	10,869.	Na 30.484
$MgCl_2$ 10.85	Magnesium Chloride, Pure Crystals. M.C.W. (46.81% $MgCl_2$)	3,241.	1,517.1	Mg 3.733
$MgSO_4$ 4.70	Magnesium Salphate, U.S.P. XI Granul. M.C.W. (48.82% m^4g)	1,323.	645.9	Ca 1.291
$CaSO_4$ 3.70	Calcium Salphate, Pure Precip. $2H_2O$. M.C.W. (79.05% $CaSO_4$)	654.	517.0	K 1.110
K_2SO_4 2.47	Potassium Salphate, N.F. VI Powder. M.C.W. (99.52% K_2SO_4)	346.	344.3	Cl 54.955
$NaBr$ 0.25	Sodium Bromide, U.S.P. XI Granular. (99.5% NaBr.)	35.	34.8	SO₄ 7.850
$CaCO_3$ 0.31	Calcium Carbonate, Precip. U.S.P. XI. Used in excess	45.	52.0	CO₃ 0.370
NaF .002	Sodium Fluoride, Pure powder. (as 100%)	0.3	0.3	Br 0.192
PO_4 .014	Phosphoric Acid, 85% U.S.P. XI	2.0	1.7	F 0.001
KIO_3 .004	Potassium Iodate, pure M.C.W. (as 100%)	0.6	0.6	I 0.0025
Na_2CO_3 - q.s.	Sufficient to adjust pH value.			PO₄ 0.012
Total - 100%	Incidental constituents in above Salts / Salts in 100 gallons Lake water other than CO₃		33.0 41.6	Total 100.000%

Fluorine = 6.35 p.p.m.
Iodine = 0.916 p.p.m. (SEE OTHER SIDE) Total Absolute Salts 14,057.3 at 100 gals. Salinity = 3.62%

106.8 gal = S.G. 1.024

Gulfport, Louisiana, arrived at Monroe Harbor. The Chicago Fire Department provided one thousand feet of hose to pump the water into the building. It was the last time Shedd used ocean water, as making seawater in-house became less expensive.

The process, however, was labor-intensive. Several times a year, aquarists made a 110,000-gallon batch of salt water, a task that took up to three weeks and involved dissolving thirteen tons of sodium chloride, along with twenty other mineral ingredients, into a reservoir of lake water.

Today, Shedd uses a commercial sea salt mix. To create four hundred thousand gallons of salt water for the Wild Reef shark habitat, Shedd engineers added sixty-one tons of the synthetic seawater mix to two hundred gallons of water and combined it with two hundred thousand gallons of freshwater. Shedd makes about three million gallons of seawater a year to replenish its exhibits.

In 1970 director William P. Braker asked the board of trustees for a collecting vessel. A seven-year-old private yacht, the *Mohini*, was purchased, rechristened the *R/V Coral Reef*, and refitted for collecting expeditions. The boat gave aquarists enormous mobility, allowing them to collect a wider variety of fishes and invertebrates. In addition, both the people and animals benefited from the amenities of a real collecting boat—large holding tanks with life-support systems, facilities for trawling and diving, and decent living quarters. The *R/V Coral Reef* served Shedd's aquarists and education department as well as several other aquariums for about a decade. Mounting electrical and mechanical problems—not to mention the damage done by shipworms on its wooden hull—led to the yacht's sale in 1982.

cheaper, faster alternative. The small live-aboard barges used for extended collecting trips in the Bahamas—while the collecting car waited in Florida—had become hard to find and costly to charter. A series of small- and medium-sized fishing boats purchased between the 1930s and 1950s had been useful but had limited range and holding space. Finally, many of Shedd's tried-and-true collecting spots in the Bahamas were turning into resorts. The arrival of masses of boaters, divers, and sport fishermen, as well as rapid coastal development and habitat decline, had chased away many species, and aquarium collectors had to go farther and spend more time—and money—to find them.

Shedd boasted the most advanced marine life-support system of its time. A press release from January 19, 1930, explained: "Fish in the new John G. Shedd Aquarium . . . will be kept cool by mechanical refrigeration equal to the melting of 450 tons of ice each twenty-four hours, or enough to supply the ice boxes of thirty-six thousand families with twenty-five pounds a day. . . . William H. Carrier, noted air conditioning engineer of Newark, New Jersey, worked out the refrigeration installation to keep both salt water and freshwater constantly at the right temperatures, varying for each sort of fish."

Right: Shedd's belugas cooperate in a mouth exam during one of their frequent training/play sessions. The original beluga group was collected in Hudson Bay, in Canada, but Shedd has since gained two new belugas thanks to its breeding program.

The next year, the board of trustees approved the construction of a new collecting and research vessel, the *R/V Coral Reef II*. The eighty-foot, blue-and-white aluminum-hulled boat had room for eleven passengers and three crew members, and was launched in September 1984. Its features include an eighteen-hundred-gallon specimen tank in the main deck, five 150-gallon live wells flanking the deck-house, and a filtered life-support system that can operate on open seawater or as a recirculating closed system. The boat has a dive platform, onboard air compressors, scuba tanks, a five-hundred-watt underwater light for night dives, and trawls, seines, and other collecting gear. It also carries two small motorized boats for expeditions to areas that cannot accommodate its six-foot draft. In addition to being available for Shedd's collecting, research, and education trips, the *R/V Coral Reef II* is chartered by other aquariums, colleges, and research institutions.

Flying the Friendly Skies

Shedd has twice collected beluga whales in Churchill, Manitoba, on the western shore of Hudson Bay. After obtaining the necessary permits from the United States and Canada to collect and move the whales, the aquarium worked with an Inuit-owned company that provides belugas to aquariums around the world. Part of the largest beluga population on the planet, the whales were collected during the brief northern summers, when belugas move from deeper water in the bay toward a shallow freshwater estuary. They were transported to Chicago by cargo jet, each cradled in a padded sling and suspended in a transport container filled with five hundred gallons of water. Since the first transport in 1989, Shedd staffers have become skilled in moving whales weighing a ton or more, often shipping belugas to aquariums around the country for breeding programs.

Opposite:
The Steinhart Aquarium in San Francisco had often exchanged regional fishes with Shedd, but in 1941, the facility gave even more, generously filling the Nautilus's *traveling tanks when Shedd's West Coast collecting trip was cut short after the assault on Pearl Harbor.*

Right:
Seamen in a small boat rescue a comrade aboard the burning USS West Virginia *following the Japanese bombing of the naval base at Pearl Harbor, Hawaii.*

War Shortages

The Bimini collecting trip in May 1941 had been unsuccessful due to unusually high water temperatures in the Bahamas and delays going through U.S. customs. Concerned, Director Walter H. Chute wrote in the board minutes for September 22: "Unless arrangements can be made for another collecting trip soon, the aquarium will have empty tanks this winter for the first time."

The board of trustees authorized a collecting trip to San Diego for cold-water Pacific fishes. In addition, the *Nautilus* would carry 539 midwestern freshwater fishes to exchange with San Francisco's Steinhart Aquarium for species from northern California. The collecting car arrived in San Diego on December 6, 1941.

The next morning, Pearl Harbor smoldered, and San Diego closed its harbor. The Shedd crew left, having netted only a fraction of what they needed. Fortunately, the Steinhart Aquarium contributed scores of additional animals to Shedd. The *Nautilus* returned with

STEINHART AQUARIUM
GOLDEN GATE PARK
SAN FRANCISCO
8-15

1,451 specimens, more than two-thirds of them from San Francisco.

In June 1942 Marineland in St. Augustine closed and offered Shedd its collection. The 249 animals were the last saltwater specimens Shedd would acquire for several years. Shedd was able to keep its freshwater galleries stocked thanks to its semiannual receipt of fishes from the U.S. Fish and Wildlife Services' Guttenburg, Iowa, hatchery and donations from both the Indiana Conservation Department and the Michigan Conservation Commission. By the end of the war, however, Shedd's saltwater collection had dwindled by 80 percent, and Shedd was forced to close one gallery.

Shedd's saltwater collection didn't begin to rebound until 1949, when the aquarium was able to make a successful collecting trip to the Dry Tortugas, and Pacific reef species were again available for purchase. Still, it wasn't until 1959 that Shedd Aquarium was operating at full capacity once more.

NEPTUNE'S
TEMPLE

Far and near left: The aquarium's architects decorated every surface and fixture with aquatic life, including a petite bronze seahorse on an entry lantern and a gold dolphin on a red-tiled façade in the old Tributaries room.

Opposite: The rotunda, shown with its eighty-foot-wide skylight, was restored to its original glory in 1999. Shedd's Caribbean Reef exhibit received a state-of-the-art renovation at the same time.

Shedd Aquarium was designed by the Chicago-based architectural firm

of Graham, Anderson, Probst & White. The firm's other local work included the Field Museum, the Wrigley Building, the Museum of Science and Industry, and the Merchandise Mart. Many of the firm's buildings, including the aquarium, have been designated national historic landmarks by the National Park Service.

An example of the Greek- and Roman-inspired Beaux Arts architecture that was promoted by Chicago architect Daniel Burnham at the turn of the twentieth century, Shedd Aquarium is perhaps the firm's grandest effort. Ernest Graham, one of Burnham's former assistants, stayed faithful to the style while making adjustments to reflect the nature of the building. The front of the aquarium features elements of a classic Greek temple, including Doric columns that support the entrance portico. And the broad staircase leading to the entrance reflects the ancient Greek practice of placing temples on platforms to distinguish them as important buildings.

The aquarium's layout follows a traditional Greek floor plan: Designed as a circle-in-a-cross, the centerpiece of the building is a great foyer with three pairs of galleries extending from a rotunda. From there, the architects created an octagon, filling in the corners of the cross to create work areas for the staff, including food storage and preparation rooms and a fish hospital. The eighty-foot-wide glass dome that crowns the one-hundred-foot-high rotunda repeats the octagon.

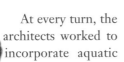

At every turn, the architects worked to incorporate aquatic touches into the traditional design. Waves roll up the outside of the dome to Neptune's trident. Sea turtles, fishes, and sea stars appear in the bronze doors, ceiling panels, chandeliers, and terra cotta trim. Chicago was a leading supplier of terra cotta, and some of the country's finest artists produced the white-glazed clay animals, shells, and other ornamentation that adorn the building. Walter H. Chute, aquarium director from 1928 until 1964, oversaw the aquarium's construction and worked closely with local sculptor Eugene Romero to make sure the sea creatures portrayed in terra cotta, plaster, and bronze were true to life.

The rotunda originally housed a forty-foot-diameter sunken tropical pool called the "swamp scene," which was filled with tropical plants, freshwater fishes, frogs, and turtles, and was flooded with natural light from the glass dome. In 1971 the pool was replaced with the ninety-thousand-gallon Caribbean Reef, one of the country's first large multispecies exhibits. To highlight the artificially illuminated reef exhibit—and slow down algae growth—the inside of the dome was blacked out and the walls above the marble wainscoting were painted dark green. Once the brightest and most elegant space in the aquarium, the rotunda was hidden in darkness. In 1999, while the Caribbean Reef underwent a renovation, the rotunda and dome were restored to their opening-day glory, with new lighting that can either highlight the architecture or be dimmed during dive presentations in the Caribbean Reef.

With their brightly lighted exhibit windows, Shedd's original long, darkened galleries are typical of the traditional European aquariums. Art museums also influenced the design of the galleries. Guests moved from one framed window of beautiful and bizarre sea creatures to another, as if they were looking at art. Educational graphics were limited to a picture of each animal and its name in English and Latin.

Years later, two developments in the way animals are exhibited would change the shape of aquariums: a new type of aquatic display facility that featured marine mammals, and the immersive exhibit, which

permitted visitors to walk through rather than around a natural-looking animal display.

The Oceanarium

The architectural firm of Lohan Associates faced several design challenges in constructing the Oceanarium: The addition needed to satisfy the spatial, physiological, and psychological needs of a variety of cold-ocean mammals and birds; it had to complement but not compete with a national historic landmark; and finally, it had to occupy land that at the time did not exist.

The only way to expand was into the lake, enlarging the circle of landfill on which the aquarium sits. On September 17, 1987, sixty years after the groundbreaking for the aquarium, the underwater cornerstone for the Oceanarium's seawall was dropped into Lake Michigan. The area for the

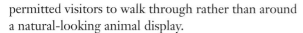

The illuminated clock and bronze skate sconces that hold nautilus-shaped shades of capiz shell recall the work of Louis Comfort Tiffany. While the aquarium's exquisite bronze fixtures are not authentic Tiffany pieces, they are masterful imitations created by the Superb Bronze & Iron Company.

new building was enclosed with sheets of steel that were driven into the lake's clay bottom. Thirty million gallons of water were pumped out of the newly created "Lake Shedd," and twenty-two thousand cubic yards of landfill were dumped in.

In order to leave the front view of the landmark unchanged, the Oceanarium was designed to fan out from the back wall of the aquarium. The roofline of the four-story addition was kept lower than the original building to allow a graceful and respectful transition from old to new, and the classical and contemporary styles were linked architecturally by finishing the Oceanarium's exterior with the white Georgia marble stripped from the construction side of the aquarium. The original thick slabs were sliced into thinner sections, providing just enough marble to cover the north and south sides of the new building.

Whereas the original aquarium building was designed as an elegant setting for nearly two hundred exhibit tanks, a significant portion of the Oceanarium's

interior is the exhibit. Guests can peer into large pools as they stroll along "nature trails" that curve through a re-created Pacific Northwest coastal ecosystem or come face-to-face with whales and dolphins at the floor-to-ceiling windows of the underwater viewing gallery.

Thanks to 160-foot roof trusses that eliminate the need for support columns, guests in the Oceanarium's amphitheater can easily view the marine mammals from any seat. From the guests' vantage point, the two-million-gallon Whale Harbor appears to flow directly into Lake Michigan.

With its well-planned architecture and unobstructed views, the Oceanarium—which also features a 475-foot-long glass curtain wall—is a wonderful complement to the original building. This addition changed the character as well as the shape of Shedd Aquarium, putting it again at the forefront of the

The original aquarium building cost $3.25 million to build in 1930. (John G. Shedd's two daughters donated the additional money.) Fifty years later, it was estimated that the price tag in 1980 dollars would be more than twenty-four million. Today, at approximately one thousand dollars a square foot, construction costs would be at least $225 million to duplicate the three-hundred-foot-diameter octagonal building of white Georgia marble.

world's state-of-the-art animal exhibits. Annual attendance shot from an average of 925,000 a year in the 1970s and 1980s to nearly two million—occasionally more—after the 1991 opening. But while the Oceanarium raised the bar for new major exhibits at Shedd, it also raised the question of how—and where—to create more immersive exhibits.

Amazon Rising

After a careful study involving architects, structural engineers, the board of trustees, an architectural historian, and aquarium guests, plans went ahead in 2000 to gut Galleries 1 and 2 to create Amazon Rising, a walk-through floodplain forest habitat and Shedd's first major exhibit to open since the Oceanarium. The exhibit incorporates the building's barrel-vaulted ceilings and exposed steel

AMAZON rising
SEASONS OF THE RIVER

Walk through the seasons of the Amazon

Take your time as you travel—you'll be exploring for a whole year.

Get ready for huge floods!

And discover how floodwaters bring a wealth of resources to animals, plants and people.

LOW WATER season

Your Amazon journey begins when the river is low.

Right: Lifelike fabricated corals on every surface and floor-to-ceiling habitat windows enhance guests' "dive experience" in the Wild Reef exhibit.

arches, opening up former work areas to create sunny new exhibit space under the skylights. With its floor-to-ceiling exhibits and flood-waters, where piranhas, stingrays, and river turtles swim above eye level, it is hard to believe Amazon Rising is still under the familiar canopy of the Shedd galleries.

Wild Reef

For the second expansion in its history, Shedd went underground. The South Wing, which houses Wild Reef and was designed by Esherick Homsey Dodge & Davis Architects, was built twenty-five feet below street level under a slightly extended south terrace. Like the Oceanarium, Wild Reef is not visible from the front of the building, preserving Shedd's landmark appearance. The compact two-level structure stacks life-support and work areas over the exhibit space, with the tops of the habitats open to the upper level so the staff can have easy access to the animals.

The public area was designed to make guests feel as if they are diving on a coral reef in the Philippines. Colorful re-creations of eighty-five coral species encrust the walls and ceilings, blurring the line between inside and outside the habitats, while only five inches of acrylic separates guests from live coral, reef fishes, and two dozen large sharks—a vivid depiction of Neptune's kingdom.

Environmental Advances

In 2004, in an effort to conserve energy, cut pollution, and save money, Shedd applied the equivalent of thirty-six acres of soybeans in liquefied form across its 144,703-square-foot roof. Unlike traditional black asphalt roofs, which get so hot in the summer that they actually raise air temperatures in large cities—a phenomenon known as the urban heat island effect—the reflective white soybean–derived polymer coating stays cool.

The decreased demand on Shedd's air-conditioning system is estimated to save ninety-five thousand kilowatt hours annually and a cool $219,000 in utility fees over the twenty-year life of the roof. The roof coating is flame-resistant and waterproof. In addition, neither the manufacturing process nor the application generates harmful fumes or toxic byproducts. The aquarium, which received a major grant from the Illinois Clean Community Foundation to help fund the project, was the first public institution in Chicago to feature a soybean roof.

THE WORLD'S

AQUARIUM

Far left: A porcelain crab and clown anemonefish live safely among the stinging tentacles of an anemone.

Left: The slow-moving panther chameleon is native to the rapidly disappearing Madagascar forests.

Opposite: Wild Reef's habitats replicate sections of the reef wall off Apo Island in the Philippines.

Animals connect us to the living world and inspire us to make a difference.

They are our most eloquent ambassadors for conservation. The beluga whales, Pacific white-sided dolphins, and sea otters in the Oceanarium, for instance, speak to the importance of maintaining a clean, healthy ocean ecosystem. And the wide variety of creatures in Wild Reef provides further living proof of the irreplaceable biodiversity that hangs in the balance as coral reefs throughout the tropics face a host of threats.

Shedd takes its responsibility to care for its endangered species very seriously. For example, most of the eighty species of coral at Shedd are propagated in-house or grown from small colonies received from other aquariums, enabling Shedd to help preserve wild reefs around the world. And its efforts to take care of endangered or threatened animals extend beyond the sea—Shedd's colorful Grand Cayman blue iguanas, for instance, are among the most endangered lizards in the world. With fewer than two dozen left in the wild, the two lizards at the aquarium are part of an international breeding and recovery program for the species.

Protecting these endangered animals remains a central part of Shedd's mission—but for the staff, volunteers, and Shedd's millions of guests, often the most memorable animals are the ones that simply steal our hearts. Whether for their beauty, size, personality, rarity, longevity, or some indefinable magnetism, certain animals through the years became favorites with the public and staff alike. Their stories are indelibly inscribed in Shedd's history.

Right: Granddad arrived at Shedd when the aquarium was new.

Opposite: The air-slurping fish really does look like a friendly senior citizen.

Adopting Granddad

AUSTRALIAN LUNGFISH *(Neoceratodus forsteri)*

Australian lungfish are native to the Mary and Burnett Rivers in Queensland, in northeastern Australia, where they're known as "barramunda." Lungfish, which possess a single primitive lung as well as gills, are among the few fishes that can breathe air. This allows them to survive seasonal changes in the level and quality of their shallow habitats by noisily gulping air every thirty to sixty minutes.

Australian lungfish have been around for one hundred million years. Shedd Aquarium's eldest Australian lungfish isn't quite that old, but his arrival in May 1933 makes him the senior resident in the building and the longest-lived of his species in any aquarium in the world.

Director Walter H. Chute wanted an exceptional display of colorful and unusual fishes to attract some of the ten million visitors expected to attend A Century of Progress International Exposition just steps from the aquarium. In March 1933 he sent a letter to the director of the aquarium in Sydney to tell him that two Shedd collectors would arrive aboard the steamer *Mariposa* on April 27. He attached a wish list of animals and emphasized that they were especially interested in acquiring a pair of lungfish.

On May 6, when the *Mariposa* returned to Sydney, the collectors had acquired a prized Australian fish collection, including two lungfish. The ship then headed to Honolulu, where two other Shedd collectors were waiting with containers of triggerfish, puffers, and other Hawaiian reef fishes. The *Mariposa* docked several weeks later in Los Angeles, where Shedd's railroad car, the *Nautilus*, was waiting to be loaded. The crew and collection arrived in Chicago just before the June 1 opening of A Century of Progress. Granddad and his mate, who lived until the 1980s, were the first of their kind on exhibit in the United States.

Shedd did not acquire more lungfish until 1994, when the University of Queensland and Australia's Sea World donated five young lungfish to join Granddad. Because of its small population, restricted range, and the degradation of its breeding habitat,

lungfish are considered a threatened species in Australia, and the government rarely allows them out of the country. These youngsters, at the time estimated to be between eight and ten years old, were donated to the aquarium to establish a breeding program in the United States.

Under this breeding program, Shedd researchers have tried re-creating the subtle seasonal changes in water temperature and pH that can put this species in a spawning mood in the wild. Researchers are also studying additional habitat requirements. Little is known about lungfish reproductive biology, and to date, the fish have not bred. But with this species' reputation for longevity, there appears to be time for Shedd's program to succeed.

Chico: A Shedd Favorite

AMAZON RIVER DOLPHIN *(Inia geoffrensis)*

Found in the Amazon and Orinoco river systems of South America, these freshwater dolphins never enter the ocean. Amazon river dolphins use echolocation to navigate, find food, and avoid obstacles in murky rain forest rivers. They use their long rostrums to poke the river bottom for mud-dwelling fishes, crayfish, and other food, which they grab with their sharp teeth.

If Shedd Aquarium ever had a mascot, it was Chico, a freshwater dolphin from Peru. His sixteen-year stay at Shedd set a longevity record for an Amazon river dolphin, or "boto," for many years.

In 1965 director William P. Braker came across a two-year-old dolphin kept in a tiny holding tank by an animal dealer in Florida. Braker quickly arranged to have the dolphin shipped to Shedd. When Chico arrived, he was four feet long and weighed eighty pounds. He grew into a six-foot-three, 225-pound adult. Chico enjoyed a 13,500-gallon pool, "trained" staff members to play games with him as they walked by, and drew forty-one hundred aquarium guests to his eighteenth birthday party in October 1981.

Chico had a funny, Muppet-like face, with a long rostrum (beak), button eyes, and a prominent melon (the echolocating organ in his forehead) that he could scrunch back, pushing the corners of his natural dolphin grin even higher. Freshwater dolphins like Chico have poor vision, so they rely on echolocation to navigate their native shallow, sediment-filled rivers. Like other dolphins and whales, Chico generated sound waves that would bounce back from an object and tell him its size, shape, and distance.

True to his species, Chico was also a deliberate swimmer who seldom rushed anywhere. Some guests, familiar with the athleticism of bottlenose and other marine dolphins, worried that Chico was ill. The aquarium took pains to let everyone know that his low-speed behavior was perfectly normal.

Chico was cared for his entire time at Shedd by senior aquarist Howard Karsner, who developed activity sessions that combined feeding, a daily exam, exercise, and play. When Chico presented his tail, Karsner gently swiped a soft-bristled brush over the flukes. Eventually, Karsner would toss the brush into the water, and Chico would retrieve it to have the rest of his body brushed.

Although river dolphins—especially males—are not very social, Chico enjoyed the time staff divers spent in the water with him, playing tag and other games. Chico lived until March 1982.

Octopuses: Underwater Escape Artists

GIANT PACIFIC OCTOPUS *(Octopus dofleini)*

The giant Pacific octopus can turn its light brown skin to red, black, or orange in less than a second with chromatophores, special skin cells filled with pigments. Arms outstretched, an adult measures sixteen feet across and weighs between fifty and ninety pounds. Newly hatched young are the size of a grain of rice.

The octopus has a brief life span. A September 1930 press release announcing a collecting expedition to Key West noted, "The early death of the octopi, commonly known as devil-fish or squids *[sic]*, which usually die after a day in captivity, has troubled aquarium directors for years. But with special apparatus and modern appliances the Aquarium hopes to keep the native species for a long time." Soon after, an American octopus at Shedd would set a record among northern aquariums by living for five and a half months.

As with so many exotic species new to aquariums at that time, the staff had to learn the animals' needs on the job. Director Walter H. Chute kept meticulous notes on environmental and nutritional requirements, as well as medical treatments, for the hundreds of species on display.

In the case of octopuses, most filtration systems of the time could not maintain the animals' water-quality requirements. In addition, aquariums had not been able to devise a secure tank latch these master escape artists could not pick, and did not yet have access to prickly artificial turf—nowadays an effective method for keeping octopuses safe in their tanks.

But despite such modern advances, aquariums must still face the reality that octopuses die soon after reproducing. After spawning, a hormone is released that causes the animal to stop eating; the female stays alive only long enough to tend her eggs until they hatch. The giant Pacific octopuses that Shedd displays typically live about two years. What makes this short lifespan all the more frustrating to the octopus keepers is that these animals are smart and trainable.

Just like marine mammals, octopuses need behavioral enrichment—interesting things to do—to stay healthy and happy. For an octopus, that might be a prey puzzle, such as a container the creature must open to reach the fish, crab, or other food hidden inside. Prey puzzles provide an octopus with natural problem-solving activities and allow aquarium guests to see the animal in action as a hunter. A male giant Pacific octopus that lived at Shedd from 2001 to 2003 learned to open both friction-fit and screw-top plastic containers.

Deadeye: Shedd's Silver Queen

ATLANTIC TARPON *(Megalops atlanticus)*

Atlantic tarpons mostly convene in tropical waters, although they can venture as far north as Cape Cod, Massachusetts, in the summer. Tarpons hunt at night, catching shrimp, mullet, and other surface-feeding fishes in their large, upturned mouths. The powerful five- to eight-foot fish are a favorite with anglers because they will fight and leap until exhausted.

Deadeye, Shedd's venerable, nearly blind Atlantic tarpon, spent sixty-three years at the aquarium, twenty-seven of them in the Caribbean Reef exhibit. At the time of her death in 1998, she was the oldest Atlantic tarpon in a zoological collection.

Deadeye's story involves one of Shedd's most dramatic collecting trips. In August 1935 an aquarium crew was in Key West collecting fishes for the salt-water exhibits. They were living aboard the *Nautilus*, a Pullman railroad car customized for transporting fishes. On September 2, the day the *Nautilus* was to head home, one of the twentieth century's worst hurricanes smashed through the Keys, killing at least 423 people and wiping out everything—including the railroad track that connected the islands to the mainland. Shedd staffers and their fishes were unharmed. But

they were stranded for two months until the ferry landing at Fort Lauderdale was rebuilt and the *Nautilus* could be removed by ferry.

While they waited, the crew endured another hurricane, equipment breakdowns, and the challenge of keeping a variety of fishes and invertebrates alive in the railroad car's holding tanks and in "live cars" that were submerged offshore. But the crew continued to collect a few more species on their wish list, including some small tarpons. The *Nautilus* finally rolled into Chicago on November 9, and Deadeye and at least two others became the first Atlantic tarpons on display in a public aquarium.

Deadeye didn't acquire her name until 1959, when she survived a nearly fatal accident. Tarpons are jumpy by nature, and she became spooked during routine exhibit maintenance. Instinctively, the powerful fish leaped from her Gallery 1 exhibit into another

tank, then another, and finally landed, thrashing, on the floor. She lost half her scales and most of her vision. Aquarists spent more than six months nursing her back to health.

Fortunately, Deadeye could still navigate, thanks to her lateral lines, the sensory organs that fish have along their head and sides. When the Caribbean Reef opened in 1971, she was one of the first residents of the ninety-thousand-gallon exhibit, and she became one of the most popular animals. Because of her limited

vision, though, she occasionally swam into other fishes and exhibit rockwork. One night in 1998, she wedged herself in some artificial corals and was badly injured as she wriggled out. This time, the aquarists and veterinarians weren't able to save her.

Sport fishermen call the tarpon the "silver king," and Deadeye was Shedd's "silver queen." Her remarkable longevity is a credit to her tenacity and to the many dedicated aquarists who cared for her during her six decades at the aquarium.

Lindy, the Flying Fish

NEON TETRA *(Paracheirodon innesi)*

Neon tetras live in the deeply shaded black waters of smaller rivers in the Amazon basin. Their brilliant blue side stripes function like neon signs, reflecting rays of light to enable them to find each other in their murky habitat. The tiny fish then band together, gaining safety in numbers by schooling.

Given how common neon tetras are in home aquariums, it's hard to imagine the excitement that was generated by the arrival of one tiny tetra on July 13, 1936. But Lindy was the first neon tetra ever displayed in this country. Thousands of people lined up on the front steps of the aquarium to see the one-inch fish.

Perhaps it was the novel way in which Lindy arrived at the aquarium that drew the crowds and reporters. Lindy had been collected in Peru and was part of a shipment of fishes that traveled by boat to Germany. Named for aviation hero Charles A. Lindbergh, Lindy was the first fish to fly from Germany to Chicago.

Lindy was one of six neon tetras sent to Shedd on the German airship *Hindenburg*. Four of the fish died of exposure to the cold during the flight across the Atlantic, and a fifth died in New York. The tough little survivor was transferred to a plane for the final leg of the trip to Chicago's Midway Airport.

When aquarium director Walter H. Chute met Lindy, he noted sadly to reporters, "It's very weak." After three days of intensive care in Shedd's fish hospital, however, Lindy rallied and went on to dazzle guests in the balanced aquarium room. Lindy was joined not long afterward by eight more neon tetras sent by steamer.

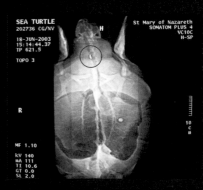

Banking on Nickel

GREEN SEA TURTLE *(Chelonia mydas)*

Greens are the largest of the hard-shelled sea turtles, with adults weighing from three hundred to five hundred pounds. They range throughout the world's tropical oceans, grazing on turtle grass and other marine vegetation. Their survival is threatened by dangerous fishing practices, coastal development, and fibropapilloma, a fatal virus afflicting green turtles worldwide.

Shedd's green sea turtle, Nickel, took to the Caribbean Reef exhibit as if she'd never lived anywhere else. On her first day in the ninety-thousand-gallon habitat in July 2003, the 124-pound turtle swam among the hundreds of fishes, ate a hearty meal of squid and romaine lettuce, and found a cozy place to nap between two elkhorn corals. Only a few guests noticed that Nickel's swimming posture was a bit off balance—head down, rump up.

In July 1998 a marine biologist had spotted the sea turtle floating among mangroves along Florida's Gulf Coast. Thin and weak, she couldn't move her hind feet to swim and couldn't submerge. A deep gash ran from the rear edge to the center of her carapace, or upper shell, unmistakably a wound from a motorboat propeller.

She was taken to the Clearwater Marine Aquarium for treatment. Yet despite months of rehabilitation, the turtle continued to have problems controlling her buoyancy and using her paddle-like hind feet, which serve as rudders and brakes. Permanently injured, she could not be returned to the ocean.

Working with the Florida Fish and Wildlife Conservation Commission, Shedd welcomed the turtle in April 2003. Shedd veterinarians gave the friendly, easygoing turtle a thorough medical exam that included radiographs at Shedd's animal healthcare center and a CT scan at a local hospital. She had suffered some internal damage from the boat strike, but nothing life-threatening. What alarmed the doctors was a round image—a coin—in her esophagus. Using a small retrieval tool with an endoscope, vets removed a nickel from the turtle's throat. The problem was solved and she had a name.

Nickel still has buoyancy problems, but her hind legs have gotten stronger with exercise, and she easily dives to the floor of the thirteen-foot-deep reef exhibit for her food.

Nickel is one of only a few rehabilitated sea turtles on permanent display in the U.S. Her presence serves as a reminder that the way we use—or abuse—wildlife areas has lasting consequences.

Protecting Hawkeye

HAWKSBILL SEA TURTLE *(Eretmochelys imbricata)*

The hawksbill sea turtle gets its common name from its hawk-like hooked beak, which comes in handy for cracking sea urchin shells or munching on rock lobsters. Hawksbills are found in the tropical Atlantic and Pacific Oceans, the Indian Ocean, and the Caribbean and Mediterranean Seas. Hawksbills are endangered due to hunting, mostly for their attractive shells.

In July 1977 a U.S. Fish and Wildlife Service (FWS) official called the aquarium to ask if it would take a confiscated sea turtle. The official arrived a little while later with a six-inch, one-pound hawksbill turtle that an aquarist named Hawkeye.

Customs officials had discovered Hawkeye in a suitcase at the Chicago O'Hare International Airport. Hawksbills and other sea turtle species are protected under the U.S. Endangered Species Act (ESA) and the Convention on International Trade in Endangered Species of Wild Fauna and Flora (CITES). The owner lacked the permits to bring a protected species into the United States legally, so Hawkeye was turned over to FWS officials.

FWS depends on qualified zoological, scientific, and educational facilities such as Shedd to care for the animals it intercepts. From the 1970s, when the ESA was enacted, through the 1990s, Shedd received more than sixty of these marine reptiles from FWS. The turtles were rehabilitated, raised to a sturdy size, and released in the same geographical area they had left.

Hawkeye's country of origin, however, was unknown. So, because he could not be released back into the proper genetic population, and because the aquarium could meet the needs of a growing sea turtle, Hawkeye stayed. Within a year, he was large—and feisty—enough to join the community of the Caribbean Reef exhibit. He was one of only a few hawksbills on display in U.S. public aquariums. He grew to an impressive size—three feet long and more than 150 pounds—and stole the show during dive presentations by nudging or nipping the diver for food.

With his beautiful amber and black shell, Hawkeye was the centerpiece for conservation discussions that encouraged guests to help protect marine species, to refrain from buying tortoiseshell (real hawksbill shell) souvenirs abroad, and to assist in conserving reef habitats. Ironically, Hawkeye broke more than a few of the reef exhibit's artificial corals as, in sea turtle fashion, he wedged himself into protective positions to sleep. Hawkeye died in 2002, almost twenty-five years to the day of his arrival at Shedd.

Gamera the Goliath

ALLIGATOR SNAPPING TURTLE *(Macroclemys temminckii)*

Alligator snappers are the largest of the North American freshwater turtles and possibly the slowest. The aquarium's thirty-five-pound common snapping turtles *(Chelydra serpentina)* have an explosive strike—far more hazardous than the larger species' slow-motion maw. With a pink, wormlike appendage on its tongue, the alligator snapper is able to lure fish in and clamp its jaws shut.

With a basketball-sized face only a mother or a herpetologist could love, this alligator snapping turtle was named for the giant prehistoric turtle featured in a series of 1960s Japanese horror movies. But if a naming contest had been held based on guests' initial reactions to this bottom-dwelling behemoth, "Ohmygosh" would have won, followed by "Isitalive."

By the time Gamera was loaned to Shedd by the Tennessee State Aquarium in Chattanooga in September 1998, he weighed 249 pounds—sixty-five pounds short of a record set by a wild-caught specimen, but heavy enough to require five aquarists to hoist him from his tank into a transport container. (The females seldom top fifty pounds.)

A commercial fisherman in Texas caught Gamera in 1982. Already an impressive 165 pounds, the turtle seemed too special to harm, so he was donated to the Baton Rouge Zoo in Louisiana, which gave him to Shedd. On a diet of five pounds of fish a week, the turtle weighed 225 pounds the next time he was put on a scale—in preparation for a 1988 contest in which aquarium members tried to guess the turtle's weight.

Few people passed the turtle's exhibit without stopping and exclaiming, although they usually just got a view of his broad backside and long tail as he hunkered in his cave. The boulder-sized animal's rare trips to the surface for air drew crowds. Visiting herpetologists often stopped by just to marvel.

Alligator snapper populations have plummeted throughout the species' range, which extends from the Deep South to southern Illinois and Indiana. Because they are large and lethargic, alligator snappers are easy targets, and they have been hunted extensively for meat. They have also suffered from degradation and destruction of their habitats, which include lakes, ponds, swamps, and the deep channels of large river systems. Although they are not federally protected, alligator snappers are listed as endangered by many states or "threatened," as in Illinois. The large ones like Gamera are extremely rare, both in the wild and in aquariums.

Oil-Spill Survivors: Kenai, Nikishka, Chenik, and Nuka

ALASKA SEA OTTER *(Enhydra lutris lutris)*

Unlike other marine mammals, sea otters don't have a thick layer of blubber to keep them warm in the cold Pacific Ocean. They do, however, have the densest fur of any mammal, which they use to hold in body heat. Pups must gobble the daily equivalent of one-third their body weight to survive and grow, while adults eat nearly one-quarter of their body weight each day to fuel their high metabolism. That's about seventeen pounds of sea urchins, mussels, clams, crabs, squid, and fish for a sixty-pound animal.

In August 1988 Shedd filed a permit application with the U.S. Fish and Wildlife Service to acquire six wild Alaska sea otters for the new Oceanarium. In mid-March of 1989 the aquarium received confirmation that the permit to collect otters in Prince William Sound in southeastern Alaska had been approved. A week later, a FWS official called to say that the permit would be delayed. The tanker *Exxon Valdez* had run aground in Prince William Sound, coating eleven hundred miles of coast with eleven million gallons of crude oil. Tens of thousands of animals—fishes, eagles, seabirds, and sea otters—were dead; thousands more needed intensive treatment to survive.

Shedd sent two Marine Mammals department staffers to the hastily set-up Sea Otter Rescue Center in the harbor town of Valdez. They were among hundreds of zoo and aquarium professionals, teachers, environmentalists, and concerned citizens who went to Alaska to assist in the round-the-clock rescue and rehabilitation effort. The Shedd staffers helped with the hour-and-a-half wash, rinse, and blow-dry procedure administered to each incoming oiled otter. They also tended animals recovering in wooden pens set up in the high school parking lot.

At the end of their stay, they were asked by center officials how many otters Shedd would like. FWS was releasing rehabilitated adult otters into unaffected areas of the sound, but the service was also looking for qualified zoological institutions to provide homes to a small number of orphaned or abandoned pups that could not survive in the wild.

Shedd received three females—later given the Alaska place names of Kenai, Nikishka, and Nuka—and a male that the aquarium named Chenik after a town on the Kenai Peninsula. At the time they were brought to the rescue center, they ranged from a few

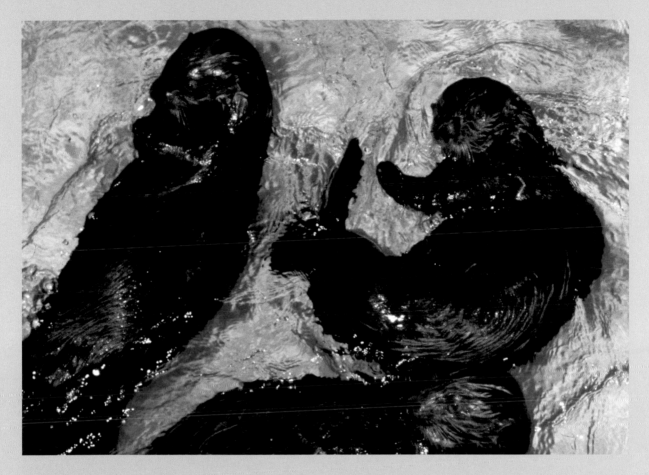

weeks to a few months old and weighed between three and ten pounds. They needed tube feeding six times a day, frequent grooming to maintain the insulating quality of their fur, and even lessons on how to float.

By the time the otters arrived at Shedd in October 1989, they were a rollicking, noisy quartet of twenty- to thirty-five-pound animals. Because the Oceanarium was still under construction, they were placed in a large habitat in one of the galleries, becoming the first sea otters on display at an inland North American aquarium. Thanks to Shedd's success in rehabilitating and raising young sea otters, FWS again placed pups in need with the aquarium in 1990 and 2003.

Kenai and Nikishka still live at Shedd. Chenik, who nearly drowned in the oil spill, suffered from seizures and other health problems for much of his life. He died in 1997. In 2001, in a breeding exchange, Shedd sent Nuka to the Seattle Aquarium in return for a young male who is the offspring of another oil-spill otter.

A Symphony of Seahorses

LEAFY SEA DRAGON *(Phycodurus eques)*

With branching flaps of skin growing from its head, body, and tail, the leafy sea dragon resembles a floating strand of kelp—great camouflage for this stiff-bodied, slow swimmer. Until recently, few aquariums had attempted to keep such delicate, specialized fish. Native to the cold waters off Australia's southern coast, "leafies" require a costly computerized system to maintain a near-constant water temperature of 63°F. In the wild they dine exclusively on tiny mysid shrimp, but Shedd has weaned them onto an equally nutritious frozen diet.

"The seahorse is without doubt the most popular exhibit in the aquarium," Shedd's director noted as one hundred of the delicate equine-faced fish went into a new exhibit. "The seahorse intrigues all new visitors, and although some people come back regularly, they never seem to get tired of watching it."

While that could have applied to Shedd Aquarium's "Seahorse Symphony" special exhibit, which ran from 1998 through 2003, the words were spoken by Walter H. Chute in 1935. In the 1930s, Shedd exhibited northern seahorses *(Hippocampus erectus)* from the North Atlantic coast. At the time, this species was becoming scarce because a blight was wiping out its eelgrass habitat.

Even now, however, seahorses are still threatened by the destruction of their coastal habitats—including coral reefs, mangroves, and seagrass beds—as well as by hunting to make trinkets and souvenirs. The greatest threat is overfishing to supply traditional Chinese medicine, which is practiced by a quarter of the world's population. Of the more than twenty-five million seahorses captured from the wild each year, ninety-five percent are for medicinal use.

As a result of the success of "Seahorse Symphony," Shedd formed a conservation partnership with Project Seahorse, an organization dedicated to studying and protecting seahorses and their habitats while recognizing the needs of the fishing communities that depend on them. Together, Shedd and Project Seahorse have helped seahorse fishers in the Philippines set up a handcrafts business as an alternative source of income (with products sold at Shedd and other aquariums); established an environmental scholarship for the children of seahorse fishers; and hosted a workshop on the care, breeding, and educational display of seahorses for zoo and aquarium professionals

from around the world. Biologists from Shedd and Project Seahorse coauthored the first manual for seahorse husbandry, and Shedd assisted Project Seahorse in gaining worldwide protection for seahorses under the Convention on International Trade in Endangered Species of Wild Fauna and Flora.

Saving Bubba

QUEENSLAND GROUPER *(Epinephelus lanceolatus)*

Queensland groupers are the largest fish in the Indo-Pacific reefs, reaching lengths of eight feet and weighing nearly nine hundred pounds. Among many species of groupers and other reef fishes, females change gender as they get older and bigger, turning into extra-large supermales. This transformation maximizes the species' reproductive ability, as supermales spawn with harems of females.

The large scar across the forehead of Bubba, the 140-pound Queensland grouper in the Wild Reef shark habitat, is a mark of how far veterinary medicine has come—and how far Shedd's dedicated animal-care staff will go.

Bubba arrived at Shedd in 1987 as a ten-inch youngster, swimming in a small cooler that was left at the receptionist's desk. Most likely, his owner realized too late that this fast-growing fish would become larger than a home aquarium could accommodate. (Shedd urges hobbyists to know what they're getting into before buying an animal.)

Bubba lived in the original Gallery 2, eventually occupying a 13,500-gallon Pacific reef habitat. When Amazon Rising replaced the exhibit hall, Bubba, now four feet long, was moved to a reserve pool. Once the Wild Reef exhibit was completed, the magnificent fish was slated to live in the high-profile shark habitat.

In August 2001 aquarists noticed pimple-like pink bumps on Bubba's head. When antibiotics didn't heal the growths, the vets ordered a biopsy. The results were negative, but a second biopsy in mid-2002 indicated a malignant tumor. Shedd doctors, assisted by an outside veterinary surgeon and veterinary oncologist, removed the affected tissue and injected chemotherapy treatments around the wound. But the cancer came back. In March 2003 the veterinary team removed a broader, deeper section of tissue from Bubba's head. The vets covered the wound with pigskin tissue to speed healing and once again injected a chemotherapy agent around the edges of the cut-out area.

Both surgeries were "wet," performed in a tub filled with anesthetic-treated water. While veterinarians couldn't keep the wounds dry and bandaged, Bubba's own mucous covering, containing natural antibodies, protected him from infection.

In October 2003 Bubba got a clean bill of health from the medical team and was moved into the four-hundred-thousand-gallon shark habitat in Wild Reef. The bulky fish with the big scar is a delight and inspiration to everyone who learns his story.

Baby Kayavak

BELUGA WHALE *(Delphinapterus leucas)*

Belugas are small whales, ranging from twelve to sixteen feet long and weighing between fifteen hundred and thirty-three hundred pounds, with up to six inches of blubber to keep them warm. Belugas produce at least eleven distinct sounds in their nasal passages that they broadcast through their blowholes, including high-pitched whistles, squeals, clicks, chirps, and even bell-like tones.

Born August 3, 1999, Kayavak was Shedd Aquarium's third beluga birth and the first calf to celebrate a first birthday—complete with cake and candle—a milestone for everyone involved with her care.

As the first calf of Immiayuk, "Immi," one of Shedd's two original beluga whales, Kayavak's odds of survival were poor. Immi was an inexperienced mother, and Kayavak was an independent baby. Yet mother and daughter bonded, and Kayavak got the hang of nursing while swimming—an essential milestone in a whale calf's development. Kayavak mimicked Immi's every move, to the delight of the staff and guests.

On December 26, 1999, Immi died unexpectedly. Her death stunned the staff; the fourteen-year-old whale had been in excellent health. Tests revealed that Immi had died from erysipelas, a fast-acting bacterial infection that overwhelms the organ systems. (Shedd has since held an international erysipelas workshop for aquarium professionals, and has received a federal grant to study the causes, prevention, and treatment of the disease, which also affects whales and dolphins in the wild.)

Not quite five months old, Kayavak was still nursing when her mother died. Luckily, she was just old enough to digest solid food. Staff members decided to wean Kayavak because fish offered far better nutrition than artificial formula. Kayavak was fed every three hours around the clock. At first, staffers put one fish in her mouth at a time. But soon Kayavak was swimming to them and taking the fish.

Kayavak was too small to be with the adult belugas, so she lived in the Oceanarium's medical pool with twenty-four-hour care and attention from staff members and volunteers. She played with a variety of children's pool toys, often with wet-suited staffers. Gradually Kayavak was introduced to the adult female belugas, and when Qannik, a male, was born in 2000, she had a playmate of her own species. A bit spoiled by her upbringing, Kayavak has sometimes gotten into trouble with the older whales. She has, however, fit into Shedd's beluga social structure without losing her spunky attitude.

Homegrown Belugas

In the wild, beluga whales are found in coastal waters throughout the Arctic—off Scandinavia, Alaska, Canada, and Siberia—as well as in the St. Lawrence River and Hudson Bay.

Kayavak and Qannik were born in the Oceanarium, the results of a cooperative beluga-breeding program involving Shedd and seven other North American aquariums. The nearly forty beluga whales living at these facilities are considered one population, and from time to time animals are moved to other locations to make the most of reproductive opportunities. This shifting among groups is similar to the fluid social groups belugas form in the wild.

The carefully administered breeding program ensures that the whales live in genetically diverse groups. Age, previous reproductive success, mothering skills, and a facility's capacity for additional animals also figure into the matchmaking equation. One or two calves are born each year among the participating aquariums.

Opposite, left, and below: Mauyak's calf, Qannik, was born in the Oceanarium. At birth, he was about five feet long and weighed approximately 125 pounds. After his umbilical cord broke, he swam to the surface to take his first breath. Then he learned to swim alongside his mom.

Five beluga calves have been born at Shedd since 1998. In aquariums, as in the wild, the survival rate is about 50 percent, with calf mortalities higher among younger, less experienced mothers. But the program is leading to more successful births through shared expertise and a growing database on beluga reproductive biology.

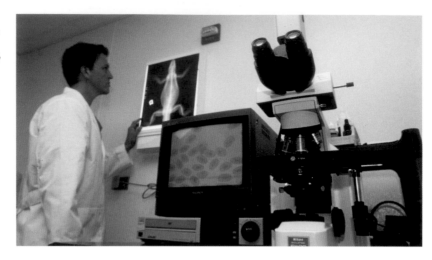

The Doctor Is In

A penguin develops a foot infection. The sharks need their annual physicals. A seahorse with a swim bladder problem must be X-rayed.

With more than twenty thousand animals at Shedd Aquarium, the members of the Veterinary Services department—veterinarians, animal healthcare technicians, water-quality technicians, a microbiologist, and a chemist—stay busy. For decades, however, the aquarists were also the fish doctors, adding chemical treatments for parasites and other ailments to the water circulating through the galleries. During the 1930s and 1940s, the average life expectancy of an aquarium fish was eighteen months. Director Walter H. Chute experimented with and refined medications for the diseases that plagued aquariums in the days before antibiotics were available and before wild, incoming fishes were quarantined. For years, Shedd also tapped the expertise of veterinarians from the nearby zoos. But with the arrival of marine mammals, the aquarium hired a full-time vet.

To provide the best care to an animal collection that now includes birds, snakes, and primates, Shedd opened an animal healthcare center in 2002 on the mezzanine level of the aquarium. The three-thousand-square-foot complex includes a hospital and pathology laboratory. A new 2,600-square-foot microbiology and water-quality lab is across the hall.

For years, part of the old lab was set aside for examinations, treatments, and necropsies, with X-rays done on a chair. This arrangement was workable when staffers were dealing with only fishes and other small aquatic animals. But larger vertebrates have more complicated healthcare needs. To maintain a high

Left: Surgeons remove cancerous growths on Bubba, the Queensland grouper, in a tub filled with anesthetic-treated water.

standard of care and keep pace with the expanding field of exotic-animal medicine, Shedd needed a sophisticated hospital.

Only a few aquariums in the country have full-scale animal hospitals, and Shedd's state-of-the-art facility is one of the largest. The healthcare center has rooms for diagnosis, radiology, surgery, and treatment. The busiest area is the spacious examination room, which includes a pharmacy. The exam table can accommodate both aquatic and terrestrial animals.

Shedd's vets do regular physical exams on the sharks and other large fishes, marine mammals, river otters, reptiles, amphibians, and birds. The schedule of preventive care spans the year. For instance, physicals for the penguins alone, including blood samples and X-rays, take two to three weeks.

The hospital includes a surgical suite, which allows the medical staff to perform operations on site rather than transport an animal to a zoo or private animal hospital. Anesthesia machines deliver gas to air-breathing animals or pump anesthetic-laced water across the gills of aquatic patients. Post-op facilities include both a "wet ward," where aquatic patients can recuperate, and a climate-controlled dry ward for birds, small mammals, terrestrial reptiles, amphibians, and invertebrates.

Shedd's veterinarians are happiest when they don't need to use all the equipment. Thanks to their expanded ability to administer preventive healthcare, many of their patients visit only for routine checkups.

Round-the-Clock Care

Even fish must sleep. But animal care at Shedd Aquarium is a twenty-four-hour responsibility. The day begins at 7:00 a.m. with the arrival of the aquarists—the men and women in the Aquarium Collections department who care for the fishes and other animals in the galleries and Wild Reef. Their first

task is doing "animal rounds" in their assigned area to check the well-being of every animal, the condition of the habitats, and environmental factors such as water quality and temperature.

The animal-care specialists and trainers in the Marine Mammals department arrive at 7:30 a.m., and by 7:40 they are in the Oceanarium kitchen to prepare the animals' meals. They bring food out from the walk-in refrigerator, examine and rinse every fish, and weigh meals for each of the whales, dolphins, sea otters, sea lions, penguins, river otters, and marmosets. Afterward they clean and disinfect the stainless steel fixtures. Meanwhile, one staff member dives with the day's volunteer divers to scrub algae or sediments from one exhibit, rotating through the Oceanarium's six pools during the week. At 8:00 a.m., the penguins, marmosets, and river otters have breakfast.

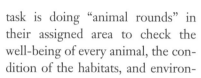

At 8:15 a.m., the aquarists work on the exhibits, cleaning windows, rearranging rockwork, performing a partial water change, and generally tidying up to make sure everything is comfortable for the animals and attractive for the guests. They also write up health reports and schedule any needed medical procedures with the veterinarians. Finally, they bring water samples to the water-quality lab for testing.

All work on the floor must be finished by the time guests begin arriving at 9:00 a.m. As the admissions staffers start selling tickets and the first busloads of schoolchildren pour through the Oceanarium group entrance for self-guided field trips or classes and labs in the Aquatic Education Center, the aquarists assemble in the freshwater and saltwater kitchens to prepare meals for hundreds of species, from sea stars to sharks. This task involves dividing live food into portions, chopping frozen fish, mixing the gelatin-based foods that so many of the fishes eat, and preparing the greens, fruits, and vegetables for the herbivorous animals. Each serving is carefully measured and spiked with vitamins, and then refrigerated until feeding time later in the day.

In the Oceanarium, the sea otters and sea lions have the first of the day's three feeds; then several people return to the kitchen to prepare the otters'

meals for the rest of the day. The belugas have their first training session at 9:30 a.m., and the penguin habitat gets cleaned.

At 10:00 a.m., the aquarists divide their time inside the habitats—scrubbing rockwork, lowering water levels to do routine maintenance, changing water in the large systems, or talking to the public. At this time, they also move animals to the healthcare center for physicals or procedures. At the Caribbean Reef exhibit, the volunteer diver arrives in a wetsuit for the day's first feed and presentation. Climbing the metal stairs to the top, he or she works with a dive tender to set up the air hoses, microphone-equipped dive mask, and feed buckets. The diver slips into the warm water at 10:30 and greets the people clustered around the reef's windows.

Before the 10:30 a.m. dolphin presentation, one of the interpretive staff members warms up the audience in Whale Harbor with a quiz on marine mammals. Meanwhile, the trainers gather in their meeting room to choreograph the order of behaviors and decide which animal will do what under whose supervision. Then they hurry to Whale Harbor, where their eager audience awaits. During this time, the sea lions' pools are cleaned.

Between 11:00 and 11:40, the belugas have a second play-and-training session, as do the otters and sea lions. Interns move tomorrow's food from the freezer room to the refrigeration room to thaw. After the noon dolphin presentation, the marine mammals staffers break for lunch

At 1:00 p.m., the aquarists load the food buckets and trays for their animals onto carts, grab the feeding charts, and head for their areas. As they feed the animals, they carefully document how much each animal eats and whether the animal seems to enjoy his or her lunch.

At 1:30 p.m., the trainers reconvene in Whale Harbor for a third marine mammal presentation. Each presentation is different. To keep the training interesting for the dolphins, the trainers change the order of behaviors and even the roster of animals taking part. The belugas have another training session at 2:00. By now the penguin habitat windows also need cleaning. As the afternoon rolls along, trainers work with different animals and prepare for the fourth dolphin presentation.

Back in the aquarium galleries, all animals are fed by 2:30, and the aquarists might turn their attention to maintaining dive equipment, assisting the volunteer diver in the Caribbean Reef exhibit during a presentation or cleaning dive, or helping maneuver animals during medical procedures. At 3:30, the aquarists make their final rounds of the exhibits and reserve areas. They end their day at 4:00 p.m.

The marine mammals staffers, however, are still going strong, assembling in the Oceanarium kitchen to do the afternoon cleanup at 4:15. The penguins are fed a second time, and depending on the time of year, there might be a fifth marine mammal presentation. At 5:00, the belugas and sea lions have their last sessions. The sea otters have a final play-and-feeding time at 5:30. Divers make the rounds of all the cetacean habitats to make sure that no maps, pens, sunglasses, or other dangerous foreign objects have found their way into the pools. Then each staffer sits down at his or her computer to write up daily records on the animals. The marine mammals staffers are on a four ten-hour-day schedule; they leave at 6:30 p.m.

But the work doesn't stop there. Water pumps, filtration systems, heaters, and chillers run twenty-four hours a day, regulated and monitored by computer, but also overseen by members of Shedd's Facilities department. By the time the marine mammals staffers are leaving, the second facilities shift has been working for more than three hours, picking up where the first shift left off. The second shift assists with the many private evening events held at Shedd, moving daytime furniture such as ticket booths out of the way, providing electrical setup, and running the Wild Reef elevators. They also make the rounds of the building—on computer, as well as on foot—to check water levels in the habitats, water temperatures, chiller temperatures, and other critical life-support parameters. This is also the time for preventive maintenance and repairs throughout the building.

The third shift arrives about fifteen minutes before the 11:00 p.m. start time for a "handover" of the

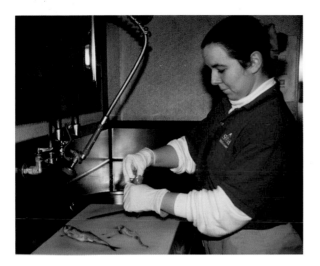

Aquarium animals can rest easy any time of the day or night.

building and to resume monitoring, maintenance, and repairs. Once the evening events are over, painting and carpentry work can be done. At 6:45 a.m., the late-night crew meets with the incoming first-shift facilities crew-members, who are already making sure all is well with life support when the aquarists and marine mammals staffers arrive to care for the animals again.

It doesn't end there. Nearly three hundred other Shedd employees in more than two dozen departments keep the aquarium running at full capacity seven days a week. From educators to research crews to ticket takers, each employee at Shedd provides a valuable service. Additionally, more than six hundred volunteers donate their time each week to the aquarium. Thanks to all these people, the fishes and other Shedd

Among the tiny poison-dart frog species in Amazon Rising is bright yellow *Phyllobates terribilis*. Toxic secretions from glands in its skin can cause instant cardiac arrest. Scientists believe the frogs get deadly chemicals from certain invertebrate prey in the wild. Captive-bred specimens, such as Shedd's, are far less potent, however, and aquarists can avoid injury by thoroughly washing their hands after caring for this frog.

Still Making Waves

Shedd continues to raise the standards for animal care and exhibition as it maintains the world's most diverse and significant collection of aquatic animals. Innovative exhibit design and high-tech life-support create more naturalistic habitats for the animals and more realistic experiences for the guests. Engaging public programs offer everyone new ways to have fun and learn about aquatic life. President and CEO Ted A. Beattie has introduced a new Great Lakes initiative to build public awareness about this threatened ecosystem in Shedd's backyard.

Yet even as it advances, one thing remains the same: Shedd is still the best, most respected, and most amazing aquarium in the world.

PHOTO CREDITS

Unless stated below, all photography credits are copyright
John G. Shedd Aquarium

Copyright Peter Aaron/Esto: 43
Courtesy of Curt Tech Postcard/Lake County Discovery
 Museum: 27
Library of Congress: 14, 15, 18b, 28, 29, 36
Private collection: 37
Copyright Doug Snower: 47
Courtesy of Target Corporation: 16, 17, 19

TEHABI BOOKS

CELEBRATE
75 SHEDD
AQUARIUM

Tehabi Books designed and produced *Shedd Aquarium: The First 75 Years* and has conceived and produced many award-winning books that are recognized for their strong literary and visual content. Tehabi works with national and international publishers, corporations, institutions, and non-profit groups to identify, develop, and implement comprehensive publishing programs. Tehabi Books is located in San Diego, California. www.tehabi.com

President and Publisher: Chris Capen
Senior Vice President: Sam Lewis
Vice President and Creative Director: Karla Olson

Senior Art Director: Charles McStravick
Designers: Mark Santos and Helga Benz

Editors: Katie Franco and Betsy Holt
Editorial Assistant: Emily Henning
Copy Editor: Robin Witkin
Proofreader: Virginia Marable

ISBN 1-931688-19-2

Printed in Hong Kong by Toppan

10 9 8 7 6 5 4 3 2 1

The John G. Shedd Aquarium, a nonprofit institution dedicated to public education and conservation, is the world's largest indoor aquarium. The facility houses nearly twenty-two thousand aquatic animals representing some fifteen hundred species of fishes, reptiles, amphibians, invertebrates, birds, and mammals from waters around the world. Situated on the shore of Lake Michigan, Shedd Aquarium is known as "The World's Aquarium." Since its opening in 1930, the aquarium's mission has been to enhance public understanding and appreciation of the aquatic world.

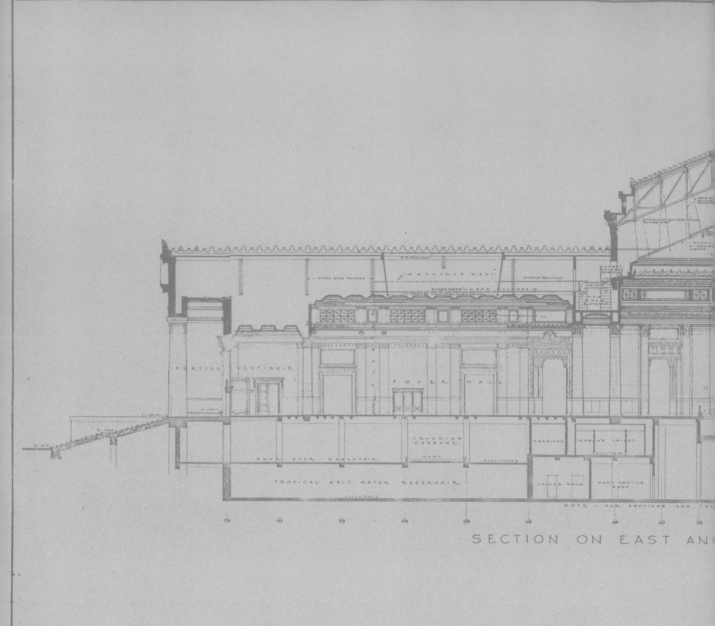

PORTICO VESTIBULE

FOYER HALL

TRUCKING
PASSAGE

CORRIDOR

WOMEN'S TOILET

RAMP

ELEV. SHAFT

LOCKER ROOM

MEN'S SMOKING
ROOM

ELEV. OVER RESERVOIR

TROPICAL SALT WATER RESERVOIR

SKYLIGHT WELL

NOTE - FOR FOOTINGS AND FOU

SECTION ON EAST AN